PICKLEBALL FOR BEC

GW00399964

Learn the 7 Secret Techniques to Beat Your Friends & Avoid to Hit the Ball Out of Bounds, Into the Net or Not Adhering to the Two-bounce Rule | Grasshopper Method

Copyright © 2022 by Ben Jilson

TABLE OF CONTENTS

INTRODUCTION

Pickleball is a racket sport that combines elements from various other racket sports. A punctured polymer ball is used as a target by players who use solid paddles. There are no restrictions on the number of players, which ranges from two to four. The ball features between 26 and 40 spherical holes and resembles a Wiffle ball. Pickleball's court layout is similar to badminton's, while the net and paddles are reminiscent of those found in tennis and table tennis, respectively.

Pickleball was created in 1965 on Bainbridge Island, Washington, as a backyard game for youngsters to play. Pickleball has been chosen as the authorized sport of Washington in 2022.

Community centers, parks, exclusive fitness clubs, YMCA facilities, and retirement homes have all contributed to the sport's growth. Physical education classrooms are another place where it is practiced. Pickleball tournaments are hosted all across the United States, such as the United States Pickleball National Championships, as well as the US Open Pickleball

Championships and Major League Pickleball. More than a thousand competitions take place each year in pickleball.

The History of Pickleball

On a Saturday afternoon in 1965, after playing a game of golf, Pritchard and Bell realized they had nothing planned for their families. No one could find the shuttlecock as they went to set up a badminton game. A new game has to be invented by the Pritchard and Bell children. Regardless of age or gender, everyone gathered on the badminton court to test their skills with a variety of balls and racquets, including table tennis paddles. To make it easier to drive the ball, the badminton net was reduced from its original height of 5 feet (1.5 meters) to hip level.

Wiffle balls were once assumed to be the best option, but it was later determined that the Cosom Fun Ball lasted longer and made for a superior game experience. A nearby workshop immediately created bigger and more long-lasting plywood paddles for the game of table tennis. McCallum's father had a basement workshop in Seattle, and the younger McCallum kept on experimenting with several paddle models. Most of the game's early players preferred the "M2,"or the McCallum 2 paddle, referred to by him as the "M2."

Early adopters of pickleball were those who lived near or were related to those who invented it. Pritchard, David McCallum, and two other friends of Pritchard founded PickleBall, Inc. in 1968. In 1972, the year they registered the trademark for the name "Pickle-ball,"the company presented its first annual report. In order to address the growing demand for pickleball equipment, the business created wooden paddles and whole sets of equipment.

Pickleball's popularity grew as "snowbirds" from the Pacific Northwest took the game south to states like Arizona, California, Hawaii, and Florida. The game has since spread across the country. A corporation called Olla, LLC, which operates under the moniker PickleBall, Inc., purchased PickleBallCentral.com in 2016.

The United States Pickleball National Championships take place every year in Palm Springs, California. As one of the event's co-promoters, Oracle CEO Larry Ellison is also a co-founder of Oracle. Since 2018, the competition has taken place at this location. It was Arizona that hosted the 2009 and 2017 competitions.

The United States of America Pickleball Association (USAPA) was formed in 1984 and reincorporated in 2005 as the governing body for the competition and its rules. Since its beginning in 2016, the United States Open Pickleball Championships have been hosted in Naples, Florida. According to current projections, there will be 3.3 million active gamers in 2019, an increase of 10% over 2016. As of 2021, the International Federation of Pickleball (IFP) was in charge of tournaments in 58 nations. There are currently around 8,000 locations in the United States where pickleball can be played.

The COVID-19 epidemic boosted the sport's appeal as a substitute for many indoor activities. When the Sport and Fitness Industry Association conducted a survey in 2020, it found that 21.3 percent of American respondents had begun playing pickleball in the previous year. It has been labeled among the "fastest-growing sports" in the United States, with an estimated 4.8 million participants. Seventy member states were represented by the International Federation of Pickleball as of March 2022; by April, eleven countries had dropped out, making a total of 59. In 2022, the state legislature voted to make pickleball the state's official sport. This is where Governor Jay Inslee signed legislation establishing a state park on the old Pritchard family courthouse.

1 PICKLEBALL EQUIPMENT

You certainly can't play pickleball without the right gear. Here are the major equipment you need to play pickleball:

1.1 The Pickleball Court

The court used for Pickleball is just like the one used for badminton. It is designed for doubles play, measuring 20 feet (6.1 meters) by 44 feet (13 meters). Compared to badminton, the front service line in pickleball is six inches farther from the net at seven feet. The non-volley line, or "kitchen line,"refers to the front service line in pickleball, while the baseline refers to the back service line.

"The kitchen,"as it is more commonly known, is a term used to describe a portion of the court that is not used for volleying. The lines are included in this section as well. Two service courts are separated by the centerline, which runs from one to the other across the court and encircles the entire court. Only the non-volley line, which separates the service court from the non-volley zone, is considered part of the court.

The net's ends are 36 inches tall (0.91 m), while the middle is 34 inches tall (0.86 m). The distance between the net posts should be 22 feet when measured from inside one post to the other post (6.7 m).

1.2 The Ball

The Wiffle ball was originally selected as the game's primary ball when it was first conceived. Since then, the International Pickleball Federation (IFP) and the USA Pickleball Association (USAP) have approved specific pickleball ball standards. This means the balls must have a moldable and durable outer shell and an even number of circular holes, ranging from 26 to 40. They need to be between 2.87 and 2.97 inches in diameter (73 and 75 mm) and 22.1 to 26.5 grams in weight. They need to weigh between—78 and.935 ounces to be acceptable. Tournaments approved by the USAP and IFP must use balls from a pre-approved list, which you can find on both organizations' websites.

For outdoor play, it is common to use smaller-holed balls, but any officially sanctioned ball can be used indoors or outdoors, regardless of the setting.

1.3 The Paddle

According to the USAP and IFP rules, paddle length and width cannot exceed 24 inches (0.61 m) and 17 inches (0.64 m). Paddles used in officially sanctioned competitions are covered by this rule (0.43 m). The weight and thickness of the material are not restricted. The paddle's surface must be completely smooth with no texturing and be made of a non-compressible material. Your paddle has to be on the approved list on the USAP and the IFP websites to compete in sanctioned competitions.

1.4 Clothing for Pickleball Players

When looking for apparel to wear while playing pickleball, there are various things to consider taking into account your taste and style. When playing pickleball, not wearing the appropriate attire might be beneficial to your performance or detrimental to your game. You should wear clothing that satisfies the criteria of being comfortable, breathable, practical, good fitting, and easy to maneuver.

The following is a list of suggested items of clothing for pickleball. I have separated the list into categories for men and women. At the very end of this list, I will also provide some suggestions for accessories that you ought to keep in mind and take into consideration.

1.4.1 Clothing for Male Pickleball Players

The following are examples of clothes that are suitable for guys to wear when playing pickleball:

Shirts

Pickleball jerseys designed for men are available in a dizzying array of hues and cuts. There is a good chance that one of these shirts will be just right for you.

Shirts with short sleeves

When playing a sport that causes you to sweat, such as basketball, it is essential to wear a shirt that allows air to pass through it. Most of the time, polyester or cotton fabric is used to make men's short-sleeve shirts. Some of them feature anti-odor technology or fabric that can absorb moisture, which helps to cut down on bacteria. Some shirts are made with mesh so that they can breathe better. The fabric of some shirts offers protection against the sun's ultraviolet (U.V.) radiation, which can be hazardous.

Polo

A polo shirt is an excellent choice when you want to look more put together while you're on the court. Polos are available with either long or short sleeves. Much like short-sleeved t-shirts, polo shirts can be constructed from fabric that wicks away moisture and offers protection from the sun's rays.

Shirts with long sleeves

Wearing a shirt with long sleeves is ideal when the temperature is on the cooler side or when you want to shield your arms from the sun. Shirts with long sleeves are practical and allow for a greater range of motion.

Shorts

Several manufacturers produce optimal shorts for wearing when playing on a court. When looking for shorts, choosing a pair that is comfortable and allows air to pass through them is important. In addition to this, check that the length is appropriate for you. On the court, you don't want to be restricted in your movement by having shorts that are either too short or too long.

Pants

Pickleball pants are an excellent choice if you plan on playing the sport in weather on the chillier side. They add a further layer of insulation to your body. You can wear them while you are warming up or even while you are playing the game. Make sure you wear shorts underneath so that you may remove them if you find that you are getting too hot.

1.4.2 Clothing For Female Pickleball Players

The following is a selection of different pickleball gear that ladies can wear while playing the sport of pickleball.

Shirts for Females

When it comes to playing pickleball, ladies can choose from a wide variety of shirt styles to suit their needs. There is bound to be a shirt that suits both your taste and the way you like to dress.

Short Sleeve Tee

You should wear short-sleeved tees on the pickleball court since they are more comfortable. They are easy to sit in and serve their purpose well.

Vests and tank tops

When the weather is warm, tank tops are a terrific choice because they are fashionable and quite practical.

Long sleeve shirts

When participating in activities in environments with a lower average temperature, putting on a shirt with long sleeves is advisable. Shirts with long sleeves that are not too heavy but still cover the arms are another option for sun protection.

Pickleball skorts for women

When playing pickleball, skorts are a terrific piece of clothing to wear. They are something that resembles a skirt but are more like shorts. They are comfortable and fashionable while also allowing you to wear shorts while providing the appropriate coverage.

Pickleball skirts

Pickleball skirts can be fun to wear on the court, but that depends on your style. They are soft and allow air to circulate freely. You can choose a skirt with an A-line cut, a straight cut, a flared cut, or ruffles from various available styles.

Capris

When playing pickleball, capris are a comfortable bottom option to wear. They are versatile enough to be worn either with or without a skirt. They offer additional protection during the months when the temperature is lower. Capris are pants that come to about the middle of your legs.

Leggings

Leggings are an excellent piece of apparel if you want to play pickleball during the cooler months. In contrast to capris, which stop at about the knee on your leg, leggings cover your entire lower leg to provide full coverage and protection.

Pickleball pants

Pickleball pants are an excellent choice for keeping you warm if you plan on playing the sport during periods when the temperature is lower. You can wear them while you are warming up or even while you are playing the game.

1.5 Shoes for Playing Pickleball

The best shoe for playing pickleball is a court shoe or a tennis shoe since these shoes are designed specifically for the court and have a tread pattern that allows for swift lateral movements and excellent comfort and grip. Remember that even the most durable pickleball shoes will eventually wear out. A good rule of thumb is that you should replace your pickleball shoes after around 60 hours of play, which is equivalent to three to four months, depending on how frequently you play the sport.

2 FUNDAMENTAL RULES OF PICKLEBALL

A court of 20 feet by 44 feet is required for the sport of pickleball. The ball is served in a diagonal direction (beginning with the service square on the right), and the side that serves the ball is the only one that can score points.

Volleys can only be attempted on both sides of the court after the ball has bounced once, and a 7ft "no volley"zone has been established on both sides of the court. You can expect the server to continue serving until an error occurs. The team that scores eleven points and has a margin of victory of two points will win the game. Pickleball matches can be played by either a singles or a doubles team.

2.1 Serving in Pickleball

The serve is done in a diagonal pattern, beginning with the right-hand service square and rotating between them with every serve. The non-volley zone is approximately

7f in front of the net; the serve must cross it and land on the diagonal court.

When serving, the server's feet should be at the back of the back line, and the paddle should always be held below the server's waist. The underhand motion must always be used when serving. It is critical to avoid bobbing the ball before launching it into the air. The serving side must keep serving until there is an error in the serve. Then, the serve must be passed to the receiving side. (But if the ball hits the net yet remains inside the designated service court, the serve can be retaken.)

The serving player has to constantly keep their feet at the back of the back line when serving. When the ball is served underhand, the pickleball paddle comes into contact with it just below the player's waist. To serve, the server has to throw the ball into the air successfully. The serving player shouldn't bounce the ball and attempt to throw it off as it bounces. The serve must cross the non-ball area, including the line, and must be hit diagonally across the court (serves that land on the non-ball area line are invalid). When serving, only one attempt is permitted, unless the ball hits the net and lands in the correct service area, in which case the serve may be repeated.

When a new game begins, the team that will serve first has one chance to make a mistake before passing the ball to the opposing team. Following that, both teams' players will serve before making an error before the ball is passed to the other team. If the side receiving the serve wins, play always begins with the team member positioned on the right corner of the court.

2.2 Volleys

When volleying, it is improper to strike the ball mid-air without allowing it to bounce. Pickleball players can only achieve this by placing their feet at the back of the non-volley zone line (7ft behind the net).

2.3 'The Kitchen'

It's common to refer to the Non-Volley Zone as "the kitchen."

Volleying is not allowed inside the NVZ's boundaries. Players are not permitted to perform smashes while they are inside the zone due to this rule. However, doing so is not advised if a ball is bouncing in the kitchen. If the opposite is true, you are allowed to enter the zone, hit the ball, and then leave the room.

When volleying a ball, it is a fault if a player walks inside the NVZ zone. This includes walking on any lines that are connected to the NVZ zone.

A player commits a foul when they volley the ball and when the paddle or anything they are putting on, touches the neutral zone (NVZ) or any lines connected to the NVZ. Even if the opposing player has hit the ball in an effort to return it, this remains the case.

A player may be inside the NVZ at any time (except when they are volleying the ball), although doing so is not recommended because it nearly invariably results in a point being lost.

BOTH feet must be reestablished outside the NVZ before a player can hit the ball once more after entering it and hitting a bouncing ball. The player can only then return to the NVZ. The "dinking"game becomes a big part of the overall tournament due to the nature of the kitchen.

2.4 Two Bounce Rule

The Two Bounce Rule is another name for the Double Bounce rule. It states that both teams play their opening shot off the bounce. In other words, the team receiving the serve must wait for it to bounce before playing it, and the team serving must wait for the serve return to bounce before playing it. You have the choice of volleying the ball or playing it off the bounce following these two bounces.

Faults

- Any action that causes the game to be halted because it violates the rules constitutes a fault.

- If the team receiving the ball makes a mistake, the team serving gets the point.

- If the serving team makes a mistake, the server will either lose the serve or be sidelined.

- When one of these things happens... (the actual rules have a listing of many more exceptions)

- A serve does not come to rest within the boundaries of the court that is receiving it.

- Any return, including the serve, can result in a ball hitting the net.

- Before the implementation of the double bounce rule, the ball was volleyed.

- A player hits the ball beyond the field of play.

- The NVZ initiates a volley with the ball.

- Before the receiver hits, the ball has two opportunities to bounce.

- It is a violation of the rules if your clothes, your body or your paddle makes contact with the net or one of the posts while you are playing. This includes touching the net with the paddle.

2.5 Scoring

When a team is serving, it will only receive one point. The serving player has to keep serving until their team makes a mistake. When playing doubles, each team member must keep serving till their team commits an error. The serve is then passed to the opposing team, which is known as a "side out." Although Pickleball is played till the first team scores 11 points, a team has to win by at least two points to be declared the winner.

Because doubles games account for the vast majority of pickleball matches, the rest of this book will be written from the perspective of a doubles player.

With the exception of the first serving sequence of every new game, the two players on the serving doubles team can play and win points until they make a mistake. This rule does not apply to the initial service sequence of each new game. Each new game starts with one partner from the serving team getting to serve. This person will serve as the server until a mistake is made, at which point the service will be delivered to the receiving team.

At the start of every side-out, the opening serve is done on the right-hand court. That person is assigned to the position of server number one (1). The first score will be revealed to be 0-0-2. The "0-0-start" signal was removed from the competition when the rules were updated in January 2016.

When a point is won, the server will switch sides and begin another serve from the left side of the court. This will continue until someone gets a point.

When the ensuing points are scored, the server alternates between the right and left sides of the court. This process is repeated until the initial server loses the serve, at which point a mistake is made.

The partner then serves from whichever side they are currently on when the first server (1) fails to finish a serve.

Until the opposing team commits a mistake and forfeits the serve, the second server will keep serving. "Side out"occurs, and the opposing team now has possession of the ball.

After the serve has been returned to the first team, server one (1) will serve the ball from the right side of the court, following the same guidelines as stated above, unless they, too, commit two faults, in which case the serve is returned to the first team.

When playing singles, the person who serves does so from either the right or left side of the court, depending on whether their score is even or odd. The remaining rules remain unchanged.

Who is the first in line to serve? Any reasonable strategy is permissible. Sometimes a specific area has its own system. To determine who would serve first, you could play a rally similar to ping pong, assume that the north side always plays first, toss a coin, etc. At the Onalaska YMCA, the side of the room closest to the curtain is served first.

2.6 Other Scoring Rules

If the full score and the server number are not called before serving the ball, it is considered a FAIL, and the serve is passed to the next person, regardless of who is on which side.

Following the announcement of the score, the server has 10 seconds to serve the ball before it is considered a FAIL on their part.

In pickleball, the player who served first in the game is always on the right side of the court while serving or receiving the ball when the incumbent team's score is even. This rule is applicable regardless of which side of the court the serving team is on. What happens if the person serving is from the wrong side? According to Rule B.6, if the ball is served by an incorrect team member or from an incorrect court, the service is considered a fault. If the issue was caused by the first server, the first service would be terminated, and the second server would start providing service from the correct position. If the mistake was made by the second server, it is considered a side out. If the game has progressed and another point has been scored or the opposing side has served, the point scored from an incorrect service position or by an incorrect server will be null and void.

2.7 Line Calls

If the ball touches any line other than the kitchen lines during a serve, it is considered "in."If the serve touches the kitchen lines or the kitchen/NVZ zone, it is considered short and defective.

The rules require you to declare a ball "in"even if you are unsure whether or not it has been scored. If you and your partner disagree on the line call, it is acceptable to inquire as to how the other team perceived the situation. What that team decides to say in response to the call is final. If a referee is asked to make a call and is available, the call stands as made by the referee.

2.8 Net Rules

If you hit the ball and it goes over the net, drops, and hits the horizontal bar, it is still in play and must be played by the opposing team.

The same thing happens, but this time the ball gets caught between the horizontal bar and the net. You must let that go and return to the point.

The same thing occurs, except that the ball rolls over and strikes the foot in the middle of the net rather than the horizontal bar. You must let that go and return to the point.

When you hit the ball, it travels across the court and makes contact with the horizontal bar on your side of the net. This is a blunder that will cost you the game.

3 TERMS IN PICKLEBALL

There are several essential pickleball terms you should be familiar with before hitting the pickleball court. Here are some common terminologies used in the game of pickleball:

Pickleballs: Wiffle balls or plastic balls with holes serve as pickleballs.

Paddle: Despite common belief, this piece of equipment is not a racket. You strike the ball with the paddle.

Pickleball doubles: A pickleball double is a two-team game in which there are four players total.

Pickleball singles: There is no second server on either team in a pickleball single, which is played between two players, one on each side.

Skinny singles: A game in which only half of the court is used by the two players, one on each side.

Non-volley zone: The front of the Pickleball court, on both sides of the net, is the non-volley zone, which is a 7-foot area. Standing at this spot, pickleball players are unable to use volleys to hit balls into the air.

Non-Volley Line: The non-volley line designates the non-volley zone and runs parallel to the net.

Backcourt: The term "backcourt" refers to the few feet behind a courtside's baseline.

Double Rule: Both sides must take their first shots after allowing the ball to bounce under the double bounce or two bounce rules. The serving team must wait for the serve to bounce before playing it, and the receiving team must do the same for the server.

Centerline: Running from the NVZ toward the baseline, the centerline divides the service court into two halves.

Sidelines: The sidelines are the lines that go down each side of the court.

Baseline: The line at the far end of the court is known as the baseline. The baseline is typically 22 feet away from the pickleball net.

Permanent object: Any anything on or near the court that could obstruct play, such as ceilings, onlookers, etc., is referred to as a permanent object.

Rally: Continuous play starting with the delivery of the ball and ending when a fault or point is recorded.

Serve: A serve is a backhand shot that initiates a pickleball rally. Pickleball gives you two serves per game. It is required to serve the ball from below the waist.

Serve outside scoring: A player has to accept the serve in order to score a point in pickleball, and you can only score a point when you serve.

Server number: The server must call their number, either "1"or "2," based on if you served first or second on your side when playing doubles. It is necessary to call out both this number and the score.

Volley shot: The volley shot snags the ball just as it is about to bounce. When the player is in the kitchen or before the first three shots, this move is not allowed.

Ace: An ace is a serve that the opposing team does not return.

Put away: A ball that is out of play for the opposition, culminating in a successful shot.

Overhead shot: Similar to a tennis serve, an overhead shot is a shot that is fired above the shoulder.

Line call: A term referring to if the ball is in or out.

Foot Fault: When your foot placement causes you to serve or volley poorly.

Face of the paddle: The paddle's face is the part of the handle that is utilized to make shots.

Approach shot or approach stroke: A pickleball approach stroke involves hitting the ball in the direction of the net.

Backhand: Repositioning the paddle before a shot

Backspin: Backspin occurs when you strike the ball with a low-to-high motion, which makes it spin the other way.

Carry: A shot during a forward swing that follows the paddle rather than bouncing off of it.

Double hit: A double hit occurs when a ball is struck twice in a single, continuous groundstroke.

Forehand: A forehand stroke strikes the player's dominant side, such as the left side for a left-handed player.

Half-volley: A half-volley is when you hit the ball after it bounces but before it reaches its full height.

Punch: A quick stroke that resembles jabbing the ball out of the air with the paddle and has a brief backswing.

Top Spin: A spin-producing swing that involves moving the ball from low to high in the air. A pickleball paddle made for a spin is what some pickleball players buy.

Cross-court dink: A dink crosses the court from one side to the other, typically landing in the kitchen of the opponent on the other side.

Lob: An extremely high shot that flies into the backcourt and over the heads of your opponents. This shot is intended to make your opponents chase the ball and move out of position.

Slammer: Slammers strike the ball rapidly and forcefully. Advanced players counter that playing this way demonstrates poor technique since they can quickly exhaust their energy.

Dink shot: A soft shot that lands in the non-volley zone is referred to as a "dink shot,"sometimes known as a "drop shot."

Poach: Poaching is the act of one team member shooting at their partner rather than allowing the partner to play. When one player is much more skillful than their partner, poaching may happen.

Bounce It: In order to prevent the ball from going out of bounds, your partner may ask you to let it bounce.

OPA! : Open rally started after a cheer was shouted following the third shot

Falafel: No. It's not the delicious Middle Eastern food! A falafel in pickleball is a shot that falls short of its full potential due to the player's insufficient force when striking the ball.

Flapjack: A shot that must first bounce before being struck is a flapjack.

The Kitchen: Another term for the Non-Volley Zone.

Pickle! : To let the other players know that they are about to serve, a player will shout "Pickle!"

Pickled: If a team fails to score any points by the game's conclusion, it has been "pickled." You definitely want to stay away from this.

Pickledome: The court where the pickleball tournament is played.

Pickler: A Pickleball fanatic who is constantly chatting about the game.

Volley ilama: An illegal maneuver in volleyball where a player fires into the kitchen.

Setup: A setup in pickleball is when a player successfully persuades another to go to a spot on the court that leaves an area unprotected by the other side.

Nice get: Nice get refers to when you hit a hard-to-reach or return ball and someone on the court says it.

Nice rally: This phrase honors all players and alludes to a lengthy exchange of shots between teams.

Dead ball: The point is over since the ball has dropped.

Unforced Error: A missed shot is only the result of one's error, not the performance or skill of the opposition.

USA Pickleball: The official pickleball governing body for the United States is called USA Pickleball. It was formally called USAPA.

UPTPR (USAPA Tournament Player Rating): A rating based only on a player's win/loss record in contrast to their opponents' relative strength.

Tagging: The deliberate use of the ball to strike an opponent.

Tattoo: The physical "mark"left by a pickleball hit on your body.

Third Shot Drop: The serving team typically hits a drop shot that lands harmlessly (unattackable) into the opposition's non-volley zone. This is because they must stand back and let the ball bounce.

Topspin: The forward (and downward) spinning of the pickleball

Transition: The transition zone is the portion of the court that lies between the non-volley line and the baseline. It occasionally goes by the name "no man's land."

4 THE IMPORTANCE OF MINDSET

Great pickleball players are distinguished from the general population not only by their physical abilities but also by their mental approach to competition. One of the most important factors that contribute to exceptional athletic performance is a positive mental attitude. A positive mental attitude can help pickleball players improve both their natural and technical skills, allowing them to focus on the competition and achieve their goals.

Pickleball players who have reached a new level of positivity in their attitudes do not appear out of the blues during tournaments. They must be constantly honed to be effective. Now that we've established that, let's talk about an athlete's mindset, including its benefits and how it develops, so we can help you improve your mental game and prepare for the next tournament.

The collection of beliefs that make up a person's mindset includes everything that influences that person's perspective of themselves, the people around them, and the world in general. Because of these perspectives, an individual's mindset determines how that individual thinks, feels, and acts in a given situation.

Because each person's history, culture, and upbringing are unique to them, it is only natural that they would develop a unique perspective that would vary depending on the circumstances they were placed in. Dr. Carol Deck, a well-known American psychologist who taught at Stanford University and is best known for her groundbreaking work on the subject of mindset, played an important role in disseminating information about the two distinct mentalities to the general public. Deck's book "Mindset: The New Psychology of Success" addressed the concept of a growth mindset as opposed to a fixed mindset.

4.1 Fixed mindset

A person has a fixed mindset if they believe their intelligence, talent, and other characteristics are natural and unchangeable, hence the term "fixed." The innate nature of a person can determine whether they are skilled or inept at a particular activity.

4.2 Growth mindset

Contrary to popular belief, having a development mentality is far more liberating. In a person's growth mindset, talent, intelligence, and other qualities are seen as malleable and may be improved by consistent effort. The Importance of a Growth Mindset in Sports and the Advantages It Provides

Both of these philosophies can be developed by an individual or an athlete at any time, in any place, and in response to any circumstance. People can change the functions of their brains and the patterns of their thinking. There are many advantages to a growth mentality, and pickleball players should be aware of these advantages and the necessity of cultivating a growth mindset.

The following are the primary benefits of adopting a growth or positive mindset:

4.3 Respect and admiration for Lifelong Learning

Learning new information and developing new skills throughout one's life is an example of what "lifelong learning" entails. Pickleball players with a growth mindset are always eager to learn new skills and improve themselves. They can recognize learning as a lifelong process and help themselves develop new skills, techniques, and knowledge that will improve their athletic performance. Pickleball players with a growth mindset are always looking for ways to improve their performance.

4.4 Career advancement and accomplishments

Pickleball players who want to improve and try new things have a growth mindset, which makes them ideal candidates for job advancement and success in the long run. A fixed or unchanging mindset will prevent an athlete from growing and will harm their career.

Learning mode is a self-regulatory capacity that helps people cope with long-term vocational obstacles by assisting them in developing self-directed learning skills. Research published in the Journal of Vocational Behavior has shown that individuals in this stage maintain a growth mindset. They can be more creative and determined by performing activities and experimenting with new methods that increase their experience.

4.5 Self-Esteem Development

A growth mindset does not only affect an athlete's performance; the athlete is also affected on an internal level. When a person believes that they are always capable of improving, despite failures and mistakes, it is easy for their self-esteem to rise. They can maintain their newly found confidence and resiliency.

4.6 Improved Training Habits

Several studies have shown that students who adopt a growth mindset develop superior study habits. Taking this into account, we could say the same thing about pickleball players. Pickleball players who are constantly looking for new ways to improve themselves are more likely to develop better training routines that are specific to the challenges they are currently facing.

According to research published in the Journal of Applied Research in Memory and Cognition, individuals who feel that intelligence can be enhanced via effort are more likely to appreciate the pedagogical benefits of self-testing, restudy and be genuinely driven to learn.

4.7 Ability to adapt and be flexible

Changes in one's physical and emotional state can be more easily accommodated by pickleball players who have a development mentality. Because of their optimistic viewpoint, they are more able to adjust to changes in their environment when they are introduced to different and unusual conditions. As a result, regardless of the circumstances, people are free to focus on advancing their personal growth. Pickleball players who compete in multiple locations or who engage in cross-training should keep this in mind.

Developing a growth mindset is not as simple as taking a stroll through the park; if it were, every athlete could easily become an elite athlete with no prior failures to their name. This, however, is not the case. There is no such thing as a secret in reality; the most important elements are consistency and the integration of a wide range of mental, emotional, and other personal aspects. According to Bola Ikulayo, a pioneering sports psychologist in Nigeria, having the right frame of mind is essential when preparing an athlete for a competition. And this way of thinking is the result of a variety of factors.

Personal variables, motivational elements, and mental factors are examples of psychological factors that must be considered to reach one's full athletic potential. To achieve success in sporting competitions, all of these components must interact constructively so that participants can arrive at a harmonious state of preparation on all fronts (physically, psychologically, and emotionally). According to a study published in the Journal of Education and Practice about Ikulayo's research, one method that could be used to achieve this goal is the development of techniques that would prepare the athlete to approach the competition with the appropriate mindset.

Keeping these factors in mind, the following are some of the most effective methods for encouraging pickleball players to adopt a growth mindset and reach their full physical potential.

Always keep an eye out for educational opportunities.

Commit to continuing your education throughout your athletic career and even after it is over. Find the most trustworthy sources of information both inside and outside of your specific sport. You can improve your skills and eliminate flaws by seeking advice from professionals, coaches, or pickleball players who compete at a higher level than you do. You can also improve your motivational methods by reading books, journal articles, or blogs about the subject. Learning is an endless process with no beginning, middle, or end.

Don't limit yourself in terms of how much you can learn and what you can study because there are numerous resources available everywhere. However, to avoid becoming overwhelmed with information, you must also learn to avoid items that are not essential to your profession.

4.8 Role Models Can Inspire You

Positive role models can have a significant impact on a person's life. Straightforward motivational quotes from pickleball players you admire or sound advice from coaches can help you improve your mental state. The importance of role models in the formation of professional identity cannot be overstated. Role models provide an example of a possible version of oneself that can be tried out and analyzed to improve oneself further. According to a University of Pennsylvania study published in the Penn Libraries, these relationships can be one-sided, in which one person looks to another for perceived similarities, or they can extend into more interaction, as in the case of a mentorship relationship.

Given the importance of following in the footsteps of others, you should seek inspiration from those who have achieved prominence as pioneers, leaders, or pickleball players in the sport in which you compete. Choose the ideal role model to look up to, preferably one who shares your values or those you aspire to emulate. They could be other pickleball players, coaches, community leaders, or even family members.

4.9 Always keep track of your progress.

It is difficult to maintain a growth mindset over time; however, there is always room for improvement, adaptation to new circumstances, and the cultivation of optimism. If you have a clear picture of your strengths, weaknesses, accomplishments, and gaps, you will be able to generate the motivation to do better the next time and achieve the goals that you have yet to achieve.

Most of the activities that players and teams engage in in the lead-up to competition (such as practice, exercises, and analysis of the event, of course) serve to prepare them for the event.

Players can establish a focused, confident, and trustworthy mindset through mental preparation, which in turn helps them compete at their maximum level.

The following is a list of the five most important goals you should strive to complete as part of your mental preparation for the tournament.

You should have faith in your abilities.

Your mental preparation should focus mostly on enhancing your level of self-assurance. Building confidence can be accomplished in various ways, including regular practice, thorough preparation, well-thought-out game plans, and a positive mental attitude. Before going into a tournament, you can boost your self-assurance by visualizing yourself doing well and going over the many reasons you have to believe in your abilities as a player.

4.9.1 Get yourself ready to deal with challenging situations.

Players get the ability to deal with any hardship as they gain more experience. This includes situations that could cause them to lose focus, confidence, or composure. Suppose you haven't been through a lot of difficult experiences. In that case, you'll need to prepare yourself for the obstacles that could influence your mentality by coming up with ways to deal with each individual.

Participate as a player to the fullest extent possible.

On game day, players must put aside any difficulties or troubles they may be experiencing in their daily lives and give complete attention to the competition. You can ease into the role of the performer by engaging in pregame rituals that assist you in shifting into the role, such as listening to music or stretching well before the game.

4.9.2 Concentrate on the Game.

It is essential to the effectiveness of your mental game what you concentrate on in the moments leading up to the game. When they are competing, we teach our players where to focus their attention and how to increase their ability to shift their attention quickly. This enables individuals to keep their attention on effectively completing the work at hand at all times, rather than ruminating on previous errors or becoming anxious about the results of the task.

4.9.3 Complete and Settle on Your Game Plan or Strategy, then Commit to It.

The game strategy is communicated to the players in almost all team sports. However, players that compete in individual sports like running, golf, tennis, and racing must devise their game plans and strategies to compete successfully. You must enter the competition with a well-thought-out strategy to which you are willing to commit fully. When players second-guess or alter their game plan, it frequently causes them to play hesitantly and indecently.

4.9.4 Self-Talk

Successful players can keep their self-confidence even in adversity by engaging in positive and realistic self-talk. They converse with themselves in the same manner, and they would work with their closest companion. They also talk to themselves to regulate their thoughts, feelings, and behaviors when competing.

4.9.5 Mental Imagery

The most successful players begin their preparation for competition by visualizing themselves doing well in the event they will soon participate. They conjure up mental images that are realistic, precise, and distinct and then use those images. During the competition, they also use images to prepare for action, recover from mistakes and poor performances, and plan for subsequent actions.

The following is a list of some effective mental tactics that will assist you in preparing for a game of pickleball:

1. Make the transition from life to sports and assume a player's position. Only think about the part you play as the player, and put all your other issues out of your mind.

2. Put aside any strict demands or expectations regarding the final result. Get rid of the pressure you feel to perform perfectly or win all the time.

3. Take the initiative and approach the competition with self-assurance. Gain complete command of your degree of self-assurance before the competition begins (self-talk).

4. Focus on the process or the execution rather than the results. Focus on the here and now, and try not to think too far ahead.

5. Perform a run-through of both your act and your game plan. Imagine yourself performing at your best and then carry out the strategy you developed for the game or the race.

6. Get your head and body in the right place so you can trust your abilities. Stop practicing so you can focus on being a performer, and you'll find it much easier to enter the zone.

5 PICKLEBALL GAME STRATEGIES AND TECHNIQUES

Strategy is essential in any game and pickleball, which is both a physical and mental game, is no exception. Here are some techniques and strategies that will help you win every time:

5.1 Maintain a Consistent Level of Deep, Backhand, and In-court Serving.

The underhand serve is one of the game's distinguishing features. Because you have just one attempt to place your serve within the proper service area, unlike in tennis, it is critical to execute the serve with extreme precision. Making the serve count is critical because it is the only shot you have complete control over during a pickleball rally (except if it's a windy day). So, the serve is the only pickleball stroke that, with enough practice, a player can master and achieve a high level of accuracy.

It's critical to place your serve correctly so that it lands in the correct service box, but it's also critical to make it harder for your opponents to return the serve so that you can gain an advantage. This can be accomplished by positioning the serve out of the opponent's easy reach of the service box. To make it harder for your opposing team to return your serve, you can use these two strategies:

1. The majority of players in pickleball have more effective forehand shots than backhand shots. As a result, you should focus on your opponents' less stronger side, which is usually their backhand side.

2. If you serve well into the service box, your opponents will be forced backwards outside the baseline, making it more difficult for them to return the ball and giving you more time to build up your next point (and fortunately, a simpler third shot for you). Although a long serve is generally preferred, serving outside the court should be avoided because it leaves you with too little room for error.

5.2 Return the Ball Low, to the Opponent's Backhand, with a Feeble Third Shot.

This is the second shot of a pickleball game, also known as the return of serve. Just like the serve, the return of serve had to be played in the part of the pickleball court where your opponents are (near the baseline but inside the court). It is essential to remember if you're up against a team that frequently drives the third shot, also called "bangers." If you keep the pickleball inside the pickleball court, you and your teammates will have time to return the driving stroke. This makes it more difficult for the opposing team to drive the ball, giving you and your partner an advantage.

However, as with the serve, even though a deep return is the general rule, you should try not to hit your return outside the boundaries because doing so leaves you with too little room for error. If you want to give yourself the most leeway, try hitting the majority of your returns from the middle of the court. Your opponents will score an easy point if you do not return the ball in time.

The return of serve should be focused on not just your opponent's weak side, which is typically the backhand side. It should also be target the opposing team's player with a poorer third shot. This increases your chances of capturing the point. You are allowed to hit the return serve on any part of the court that belongs to the opposing team. This allows you to concentrate your attention on a specific player in the game. As a result:

- With your return of serve, aim for the back of the court.

- With the weaker third shot, try to score points against the opposing doubles team member; and

- Because they are a weaker player overall, target their area of weakness (which is likely their backhand side).

After perfecting the deep return of serve, you should also look at these extra pickleball tips:

The majority of pickleball points are earned along the Non-Volley Zone Line (also called the Kitchen Line). Due to this fact, it is critical to make as much progress as possible toward the line denoting the non-volleyball zone. After finishing your return of serve, you should be able to reach the line denoting the non-volleyball zone as soon as possible.

If you're having trouble getting into the Non-Volley Zone Line, try a return of serve with a higher arc, also known as a lob return of serve. It can assist you in getting into the zone faster. As a result, you will have more time to reach the line denoting the non-volley zone. However, in both of the following scenarios, this tactic should be used with caution:

- On windy days, because the wind can throw your shots off balance and even take them outside the boundaries of the court

- When playing against bangers, keep in mind that lob returns of serve have a high bounce, making it easier for bangers to smash drives (unlike a low return of serve which is underneath the pickleball net, where the bangers must hit the ball, which may throw it out of the court).

You might want to experiment with different ways of returning the serve. As a result, your competitors will have a more difficult time making a shot. For example, you could slice your return of serve (this means hitting it with a backspin). When you slice on the serve return, you should:

- Make it more difficult for your opponents to make shots due to the spin.

- Since the backspin can make the pickleball move at a slower rate, you and your partner should be given more time to reach the line denoting the non-volleyball zone.

- Keep the pickleball at a low height when it touches the pickleball court (instead of a topspin, which usually gives the ball a higher bounce).

If your team is playing against a team with players that like poaching, which is when one player charges the pickleball net and takes their next shot (the fifth shot) in front of their team member, you should try giving the pickleball to the poacher to prevent that player from charging the pickleball net. If you keep the pickleball and return it to the poacher, they will have no choice but to hit the third shot, and you will have kept them on the court.

5.3 Pay Attention to Feet Movements & Ensure Knees are Bent

This tactic may appear easy, however, it is harder than you think, and the majority of pickleball players do not employ it regularly.

Your feet are extremely important when executing your shot. So, in order to hit the pickleball in front of you, you must move your feet and reposition your body (which brings us to our next pickleball strategy tip!). Get low and bend your knees to:

- Hit pickleball low balls more effectively (this is a critical goal on pickleball courts - maintain the pickleball at a low height)

- Use your leg muscles, which are the strongest muscles in your body.

Then, after convincing yourself, move your feet and budge your knees. The difference it makes in how you execute your shot will astound you!

5.4 Keep an Eye on the Pickleball Game and Try to Make Your Shots From the Front of the Court.

The first pickleball rule is to keep an eye on the ball as it strikes your paddle. Another straightforward pickleball tip that is usually disregarded is that there are numerous distractions on the court. One shot at a time, and maintaining focus on the shot you are shooting, are crucial. Because of this, you should pay attention to the pickleball striking your paddle and ignore everything else in the game, including your partner, the next shot, spectators, and the other player's paddle.

To maintain an eye on what is occurring on the court, ensure that you are getting the pickleball in front of you. Shifting your feet is the first step to hitting the pickleball out in front of your body, as was previously described. You will put yourself in a position to succeed if you hit the pickleball out in front of your body. In order to make fewer pickleball mistakes, you should work on your technique. To avoid overswinging and to be prepared for the following shot, keep your swing somewhat compact. Put yourself in a position to advance, and if you are unable to do so, remain at the Non-Volley Zone

Line, where the majority of the points are scored. Observe the pickleball as it makes contact with your paddle.

5.5   Make Sure You're "Pickleball Ready"By Having Your Paddle Ready to Go.

You should be in the "Pickleball Ready"position while starting the transition up the pickleball court to the Non-Volley Zone Line. Pickleball Ready is made up of these components:

- A shoulder-wide distance between each foot;
- Bend your knees, compress your torso, and keep your weight evenly distributed between the balls of both feet.
- Paddle with your front facing forward or back facing a 10 or 11 o'clock position (or 2 or 1 o'clock if you're left-handed). You can also paddle with your back to the water.
- Paddle forward while keeping your head up.

Since the action in pickleball can be so fast, you must be in the "Pickleball Ready"stance before approaching the pickleball net. Holding your pickleball paddle high in front of your body gives you the best chance of reacting to a fast-moving ball. As a result of not having to complete as many tasks, your reaction time will improve. For example, you won't need to lift your paddle to hit the pickleball because it will be in the correct position.

You should also be prepared for the return of pickleball at any time! Even if you believe you hit a nice shot, you should not relax just yet; you must be prepared for the pickleball to return.

5.6 Choose Your Shots Carefully and Be Willing to Stick With Them

A player's ability to win or lose a pickleball game depends heavily on their ability to choose their shots wisely, play the higher percentages, and choose where to stand on the pickleball court. Having said that, it is crucial to make decisions promptly and then completely commit to putting them into action.

Pickleball players frequently fall into error because they second-guess themselves or alter their thoughts about the shot they should be taking while playing the game. Making a decision about a shot takes just a fraction of a second. If you decide to alter your mind, you run the risk of making a mistake since you won't allow yourself enough time to make changes.

Therefore, pick a shot and stay with it through the entire round. Instead of placing less than half of one's eggs in the basket of a "great"option, it is preferable to place all of one's eggs in a "questionable"choice.

5.7 Exploit Both Your Own and Your Opponents' Areas of Weakness.

One of the essential elements of a good pickleball strategy is to take advantage of your strengths while exploiting the opposing team's weaknesses. For example, let's say you have a good drive and powerful movements and your opponents have an excellent soft game and a fantastic dinking game, you should endeavor to drive the pickleball more frequently and faster. Avoid dissenting demonstrations. If your opponent has a bad overhead shot or poor mobility, try to lob them if you have a nice lob. You should strive to lob your opponents if you have a decent lob. If you observe that your opponents' backhand drives aren't as strong as their forehand drives, target them with your strokes. You should be conscious of your strengths and exploit them on the pickleball court. Discover your adversaries' flaws and exploit them!

5.8 Show Some Restraint

Pickleball players need to have an extraordinary level of patience. One of the most crucial abilities a player may possess on the pickleball court is patience, but sadly, many players lack it. The pickleball player who initially speeds it up frequently loses the point on the pickleball court because the opponent may respond more quickly and effectively than the pickleball player did. It's essential to be patient, allow the point progress, and only go after the pickleball when the shot is accessible (for example, the pickleball is above the net or at the net).

Be tolerant! Go after the pickleball that can be hit at the net or above the net, and stay away from the pickleball that cannot be hit, which are those below the net.

5.9 Constantly Maintain the Pickleball at a Low Height.

One of the most difficult pickleball techniques to master is the capacity to maintain the pickleball at a low height (keeping it over the net). If you play a low pickleball, your opposing team won't be able to seize the initiative and make an aggressive stroke. For instance, if your opponent's serve return is weak, you can expect them to respond with a drop shot instead of a drive. The result of a low shot near the boundary between the Volley Zone and the Non-Volley Zone is a dink rather than a rapid volley. Your opponents will hit up on the pickleball if you play it low, which should cause them to pop up and let you take an offensive, fierce shot. If you play it low, your opponents will also hit up on the pickleball.

You and your partner should try to keep the pickleball at a low height when playing doubles pickleball. To do this, think about your paddle's angle and the pace at which you are playing a pickleball game at various heights.

Paddle Direction:

- The pickleball will rise higher if the paddle is held at an open angle to the sky.
- If the paddle angle is close to vertical or parallel to the net, the pickleball will have less height.

The Speed of Your Shots:

- Pickleball should be played more slowly, with an open paddle angle to hit the ball. You will be able to keep the pickleball at a lower height and inside the pickleball court's boundaries because of the slower speed.

- Try increasing the speed of the pickleball and striking it down the pickleball court when employing a closed paddle angle to hit down on the ball.

Ensure the pickleball is low, be patient with your opponents, and go in for the kill when they pop it up!

5.10 Communicate

One of the most crucial pickleball methods you can employ to improve your chances of succeeding in doubles play is open communication with your partner. You should communicate with your teammate throughout the rally and between shots. Examples of crucial game decisions include debating who should take pickleball that hits the middle of the court, who should run down the lob, and whether to call "OUT" or "BOUNCE IT!"when a shot is going out of bounds.

Additionally, while waiting between points, you and your friend should converse. You should inform the opposing team, for instance, if you decide to alter your plan or if one of you finds a weakness in the other team. Last but not least, chat with your partner so that you can encourage one another. Fantastic shot! Move along! This is especially important if the opposing side picks on your lineup's "weaker"member. It is your duty to support your partner and become involved in the game to assist diffuse any pressure that might be there if you are the player who is not being targeted. You should make an effort to influence your partner positively when playing pickleball. Positive reinforcement tends to elicit more positive responses from people than negative ones.

5.11 Allow the Out Balls to Be Released

It doesn't matter if it's a singles or doubles pickleball; letting the out-of-bounds balls go is one of the most important skills you must have in pickleball. This is particularly crucial to bear in mind when playing pickleball against opponents who prefer to drive the ball. Keep your eyes peeled for our balls, please! Duck and dodge the balls to avoid them. Don't help your opponents stick to their stance on the issue.

To improve your ability to spot balls that are outside of the boundary, take into account the following advice:

Share Information with Your Partner: It is best to work with your opponent to locate the balls because two minds are better than one. If you see a ball out, shout and cry "NO!" or "LET IT GO!" or "BOUNCE!" at your companion.

If your opponents are hitting a pickleball at you at a rate roughly chest or shoulder height, you should let them go. Most likely, the drive of your rivals is dead. This is important when the opposite team takes the pickleball from the line designating the non-volley zone.

Focus on the Height at Contact: If one of the opposing players drives a ball that goes below the net, you might want to consider letting it go. This is because the opposing player has to hit up on a pickleball that is low to the ground to put it above the net. If your opponents hit the pickleball higher than it, they will likely send it on a trajectory that will send it outside of the playing area.

Playstyles: As you and your opponents play a few points together, you should try to assess their playstyles. Do the pickleball players you're up against typically hit the ball hard on each shot? When your opponents reach a specific location on the pickleball court, are their drives going very high and flying out of bounds? Observe any patterns that would aid you in anticipating and locating the balls.

Body Language: You should also pay close attention to your opposing team's body movements and paddle position in addition to their playing style. For instance, if your opponent's paddle face is closed or flat and they have a large backswing, you will likely receive a drive. These tips enhance your game and accurately forecast strokes, including out balls.

Remember that out balls should be permitted to leave the field of play. You and your partner will easily rack up points whenever you strike out a ball. You retain your adversaries at the point when you hit an out ball; therefore, you should aim to prevent doing that.

5.12 Dink Crosscourt

To prevent your opponents from getting the initiative and attacking with a strong stroke, it is crucial to maintain the pickleball low, as you will recall. Dinking abilities are crucial if you want to keep pickleball at an amateur level.

Try to make most of your dunks from the other side of the court whenever you can (instead of straight or in the center of the court). The crosscourt dink allows you a lot of room for mistakes. This is because a crosscourt dink will pass over the middle, lowest portion of the pickleball net.

You'll be making contact with a natural angle.

You will have extra room on the court to play on (instead of a straightforward dink).

Since the crosscourt dink is a more forgiving shot, you do not have to be so precise with it. This means that you must dedicate yourself to mastering the crosscourt dink, and you should probably aim to make between 70 and 80 percent of your dinks crosscourt.

However, it's important to remember that not every dink needs to be played crosscourt. You have to continually alter your dinks and several other shots, like the an offensive lob, to maintain an unusual pickleball strategy. A crosscourt dink is an incredibly hard move with an extremely low success rate. This is particularly true when you find yourself in a challenging circumstance, such as when the opposing team pulls you out wide with a hard dink. As a result, you should consider resetting the pickleball with a simple and quick dink if you find yourself in a challenging scenario and off balance. But be on the lookout for an Erne played by one of your rivals! Ensure you hit the dink somewhat in the center but out of your opponent's reach.

5.13 Play the Ball Above the Pickleball Net, Within the Lines, and Primarily in the Center of the Court.

The secret to winning a pickleball game is to hit the ball above the pickleball net and within the lines of the pickleball court. Whether you are playing pickleball in pairs or alone, this is true. (How I wish it were that easy, though!) The bulk of your pickleball court strokes should be sent straight down the middle, except for dinks, most of which should be directed across the court. This is a straightforward tip that can help you reach this goal.

An adage states, "the answer is down in the middle." This is usually the case since pickleball players have the biggest margin for error in the middle of the court. This is because the net is at its lowest point in the center of the court, which enables players to miss the ball to the left or right without it leaving the court and yet maintain it in play. Down-the-middle shots can be advantageous when there is a wide space between you and your opponent(s) or if you can get your opposing team to argue about who should take the middle shot.

It would be best if you aimed for the foot in the center of the pickleball court on your opponent's backhand side in addition to the middle of the pickleball court itself. This is yet another piece of good pickleball advice that I first learned. If both you and your opponent are right-handed, you should aim for their left heel on the pickleball court's right-hand, even side. This is because right-handed athletes typically use their stronger hands to strike the ball. Your left heel would be the foot on the backhand side if you were to stand in the middle of the pickleball court.

6 DINKING STRATEGIES AND TECHNIQUES

In doubles pickleball, dinking occurs most frequently when all four players are standing on the line denoting the Non-Volley Zone. Assuming that you have mastered the procedures necessary to smash the perfect pickleball dink, the next question is how to maximize the effectiveness of your dink stroke. You and your companion put in a lot of effort to get to the Kitchen line (since the majority of points are won there!), but the question now is how you win the point.

Pickleball is not only a physically demanding game, but it is also a mental challenge, which is why strategy is of the utmost significance in this sport. This is especially important to keep in mind whenever you are locked in a dink war with one of your opponents when playing doubles pickleball. What pickleball strategy can you utilize to give yourself the best chance of winning dink clashes against your opponents?

6.1 Pickleball Dinking Strategies

6.1.1 Scoop the Pickleball out of the air as soon as possible.

The pickleball should be struck as soon as it is released from the air while dinking at the Kitchen line. This will allow you to exert more pressure on your opponents as it will reduce the amount of time they have to respond to your shots and will reduce the amount of space they have to position their shots. Additionally, by removing the pickleball from the air, you will be able to reduce the likelihood of your opponents hitting the ball at an angle or getting an odd bounce as a result of the spin they placed on the pickleball. In addition, by removing the pickleball from the air, you will stop it from getting to your feet, which is a more challenging shot to respond to and hit an unattackable shot off of. Taking the pickleball out of the air will also help you win the game. In light of this, you must avoid at all costs picking up the pickleball when it is in the air. By overextending yourself by taking shots out of the air, you risk breaking your mechanics and making less aggressive dinks and more errors. If you don't overextend yourself, you can take shots out of the air without breaking your mechanics.

You have two alternatives available to you if you are unable to retrieve the pickleball from the air:

Consider Taking a Step Back: If you want to hit a better shot when the pickleball is at its highest point after the bounce, you can take a step back.

Maintain Control of the Line: If you can maintain control of the line (more on this in the following tactic!), you may want to take the shot off of the short hop or shortly after the ball has bounced. You can still achieve the goal of minimizing the amount of time your opponents have to respond to your shot if you take the shot within a reasonable amount of time after the bounce has occurred. Instead, you may wait until your opponents' dinks are at their highest points off the bounce, and then hit a more aggressive stroke when the pickleball is in its highest position. This would work if the pickleball were a dink.

6.1.2 If You Feel the Need to Take a Step Back, It Is Okay to Do So

As was mentioned in pickleball tactic number one, you should strive to keep your feet at the line denoting the Non-Volley Zone. Your opponents will have more room to place dinks and more angles to hit better dinks if you step back, more court space to place dinks if they step back, and it will be more difficult for you to hit dinks because you will be further away from the pickleball net if you step back. If you step back, you will expose your feet, which will give them an easy target to apply pressure. In addition, you will provide your competitors with additional time to respond to a shot, which is exactly the opposite of what you want to happen. Therefore, make every effort to keep your feet inside the kitchen line.

In light of those tips mentioned above, if your adversaries hit a superb shot at your feet or possibly even a fastball to which you want additional time to react, do not be afraid to take a modest drop step backward off the line denoting the Non-Volley Zone. This will buy you some additional time to respond to the shot that your opponent takes. Additionally, you might be able to hit a more aggressive shot off of a dink that bounces, particularly one that bounces relatively high. This is especially true if the dink bounces higher.

If you step back, ensure that once you hit your shot, you quickly step back within the Non-Volley Zone line and stay there until the end of the rally. You must regain your position at the front of the queue and maintain it.

6.1.3 Take the initiative and exert pressure whenever you get the chance.

You can choose from various dinks when you are in the Kitchen line. The easiest way to get the pickleball back over the net is to use a non-purposeful dink, which is a straightforward dink. You can also use intentional dinks, which are played to be more aggressive and pile on the pressure of your rivals. If a dink has a lot of spins, a lot of speed, or a lot of sharp angles, it's considered an aggressive dink. Aggressive dinks can also be dinks with strong placement.

The shot your opponents hit at you will impact your decision-making about the selection and placement of your shots. For instance, if your adversaries hit a dink that was not intended for any particular reason, you may be able to hit a dink that is more aggressive and intended for a certain purpose back to them. An aggressive dink from the other team may leave you and your partner vulnerable. If this happens, you may need to hit back with a less aggressive and passive dink.

When you get the chance, you should aim to be aggressive and pressure the opponent using your dinks. You may accomplish this, as was said above, by adding spin, which can take the form of slice or backspin, topspin, or even side spin. When you slice the ball or do a backspin dink, the pickleball will have a backspin, which will cause it to skid or skip when it touches the pickleball court. The topspin dink, on the other hand, will spin toward your adversaries, which will help the pickleball to produce some pace and take a bigger bounce off of the pickleball court when it is hit. A pickleball hit with a side spin will go in the direction of the spin and may result in some unusual bounces off of the pickleball court. Other methods of applying pressure include hitting your dink with additional speed or pace, which is easiest to do when hitting a dink with topspin, hitting your dink to have a strong angle to take your opponents off the court, or hitting your dink in some other aggressive placement, such as hitting your dink down at your opponents' feet. All of these methods are examples of aggressive placement.

6.1.4 When your opponents hit an aggressive dink, you shouldn't try to go for too much of it yourself.

You may need to hit a passive or defensive dink back to your opponents to relieve pressure. This could mean hitting a dink with less spin, less speed, less angle, or less placement. Your goal will be to effect a passive or defensive dink as it prevents opponents from responding with a strong hit. The idea is to make it difficult for the person on the other team to hit the ball well so that you can play it.

When you're under pressure and trying to hit a defensive dink, you shouldn't go for too much. Instead, you should concentrate on hitting an unattackable dink that (a) lands reasonably close to the pickleball net on your opposing team's corner of the pickleball court and (b) has a low bounce off the pickleball court. If you do this, your opponents will have a hard time getting the ball back to you. Since the pickleball travels only a short distance and has a low trajectory, your opponent will have more difficulty hitting another attacking stroke off of these dinks.

6.1.5 Change the order of the dinks and shake things up

When dinking, it is essential to change the pattern of the dink, maintain an unpredictable state, and move it about. As a result, you'll want to experiment with different combinations of spin, speed, angle, and depth while using your dinks. The more you can surprise your opponent, the more probable you will derail their pickleball strategy and leave them perplexed on their side of the court.

These are some common spots where you might hit your dink:

Crosscourt Dinks: The most common kind of dink is the crosscourt dink (instead of straight or in the center of the court). The crosscourt dink gives you the best margin for error because of the following:

The center of the net is the thinnest area.

You're making contact with a natural angle.

You have extra space to dink into on the side of the court where your opponents are situated in the Non-Volley Zone.

Dinks Down the Line: Despite a crosscourt dink's advantages, you shouldn't make a crosscourt dink on every dinking shot. Instead, you should focus on making dinks down the line. This is especially true when you consider that continually moving crosscourt may pressure you to improve your skills with each subsequent stroke. Additionally, you want to maintain an air of mystery! If you want to keep your opponents moving and prevent them from cheating to one side of the pickleball court, you might want to consider going down the middle of the pickleball court or along the line on your corner of the pickleball court. When you are under a lot of pressure, it is typically simpler to make a successful shot by dunking the ball down the line as opposed to dunking the ball across the court.

In light of this, you should think about employing down-the-middle and down-the-line dinks to stay in points if you are unable to return hard or well-placed shots by your opponents with crosscourt dinks. These dinks can be used wherever on the court. This is especially important to keep in mind if your opponents are playing powerful and aggressively angled crosscourt dinks that yank you off the pickleball court and put you out of position. You may discover that it is simpler to lightly tap the pickleball over the net in front of you rather than hit a shot at an acute angle back across the pickleball court. This is because the net is lower in front of you. Finally, when you see wide court space on the pickleball court due to your opponent's over-shifting, you should think about going down the line on your side of the court. However, you need to pick your opportunities wisely because your opponent might be anticipating and ready for your down-the-line shot (for example, expert pickleball players might try to hit you with an Erne shot!).

Dinks in the Middle: The usage of dinks in the centre is a great way to confuse your opponents and perhaps get them fighting over the pickleball. Middle dinks may also be used to make your opponents fight over the pickleball. This is especially important to remember while you are competing against rivals who have only recently begun competing against one another in the same game. Middle dinks are another beneficial shot to use when attempting to open up the pickleball court. Take, for instance, a situation in which you are playing doubles pickleball and take a dink to the center of your opponents. Both of your rivals move one foot closer to the center of the field. You now have more leeway to hit the pickleball toward the sidelines when your opponents return it to you in pickleball because they both moved toward the middle of the court. This gives you an advantage in the game. After then, your adversaries will proceed toward the sideline to return the pickleball to the court. As a result of one of your competitors moving toward the sideline, you now have even more space in the middle of your opponents. Do you see a trend here? You can gain access to other areas of the court by making good use of the middle dink. In conclusion, if your opponents are relatively advanced pickleball players, you should try to avoid an Erne from them by using middle dinks as much as possible.

Dinks to Your Opponents' Feet: It is difficult for your opponents to aggressively hit a pickleball at or near their feet, making dinks to your opponents' feet an excellent way to create pressure. Dinks can be shot crosscourt, along the line, or down the middle of the court. Because of this, your competitors won't be able to hit the pickleball out in front of their bodies like they normally would.

Most pickleball players have dinks to backhands, which are strokes significantly weaker than their forehand shots. As a result, dinking the ball to a pickleball player's backhand is a typical tactic that may be quite effective on the pickleball court.

Again, the most important thing is to be unpredictable and to switch things up!

6.1.6 Exercise Patience

Dink wars are difficult and demand a lot of patience to win. As the dink fight continues, the level of pressure will continue to increase, and it is natural to feel the need to release this pressure by either choosing a winner or speeding up the point in some other way to escape the dink battle. But suppose you speed up a shot that can't be attacked. In that case, you'll probably end up losing the rally because you'll either hit the pickleball into the net, hit the pickleball out of bounds, or hit the pickleball at your opponents so they can easily counterattack. Use just those shots that can be attacked in return. Resist the impulse to attack a shot your opponents have taken that cannot be attacked. Be patient and continue to develop the point by hitting great shots that put pressure on your opponents to hit a shot that is less than perfect. This will put you in a better position to win the point.

6.1.7 Collaborate closely with your co-worker to achieve your goals as a team.

When playing pickleball doubles, you and your partner are required to work together as a cohesive unit. You won't be successful if you don't collaborate with your teammate to solve the problem. You and your partner will need to keep in mind two essential requirements for the team to function effectively:

Stay in Line With Your Teammate : When you and your partner are dinking at the Kitchen line, you will follow the pickleball in tandem with your partnerThe distance between you and your companion at the kitchen line is normally six to eight feet. Imagine a thread that runs between six and eight feet from one of you to the other of your partners. Should you move, your partner ought to move as well. If your partner moves, you should follow their lead and do the same.

Communicate: If your opponents hit the pickleball along the middle of your side of the court, you and your partner will be able to go after the pickleball. If this happens, your opponents will have hit a good shot. On the other hand, you and your partner will have a chance of colliding with each other and breaking paddles if you do so. Due to this fact, communication is necessary to win doubles pickleball. On the pickleball court, it is important to maintain communication with your partner by saying "mine", "me", "You.", "I got it" and "Yours" Additionally, as a matter of thumb, the player who has the forehand that is down the middle should be the one to take the shots that are down the middle. This is because forehand shots are typically more powerful and consistent than backhand shots.

7 SHOTS TO USE IN PICKLEBALL

Experimenting with different shots is one of the most enjoyable aspects of playing pickleball. Don't forget that mastering the fundamental shots is essential especially if you are just starting as a player. It is a very significant component of the arsenal you possess. Just make sure you keep working on them!

7.1 The Fundamental Moves

A "shot" is not the same thing as a "stroke." The way you hit the ball is referred to as a stroke in the game of pickleball. The shot is the next action that takes place after a stroke has been made. A stroke is founded on principles and is more comprehensive, whereas a shot is more narrowly focused.

In pickleball, there are three fundamental strokes that you can use.

7.1.1 Groundstroke

Any shot taken after the ball has already bounced once is considered a groundstroke. The most shots you will attempt in pickleball, such as dinks and groundstrokes, will fall into the latter category.

7.1.2 Volley

To put it another way, a volley can be defined as a shot that is executed before the ball makes contact with the ground. If any part of your body touches the ball when it has not bounced, it counts as a volley! Volley shots are usually more aggressive than other types of shots. The overhead smash is a common type of volley and also happens to be my personal favorite. Remember that you are not allowed to play volleyball in the kitchen!

7.1.3 Dink

A drink can only be executed at or very close to the net. Dinks are defined primarily by the fact that they are prepared in the kitchen, have a very low rebound, and are only narrowly successful in clearing the goal net. During a game of pickleball, players have access to a huge variety of different dink shot options to choose from.

It is necessary for me first to describe the objective of the dinking game before I can go on to explain the dinking strategy.

The dinking game in pickleball is structured in such a way that its sole purpose is to ensure that your opponent, and not you, makes the error. The dinking game has a very straightforward and easy-to-understand format at its core. It consists of nothing more than you and your opponent taking turns gently hitting the ball back and forth over the net. However, this isn't just done for the sake of having fun. A dink shot allows the ball to land gently on the opposing side. Because the ball will bounce low off the ground, the opposing team can't hit it with enough force to get it over the net, and this will increase the likelihood that they will win the point. They will be unable to carry out this plan as a result of the dink. A dink will very infrequently earn you a point for your team, but it will almost always cost you a point.

So, how exactly does one execute a dink stroke? as gently as it is physically possible to do so.

The dinking motion is delicate but exact. You won't want the opposing team to send the shot to you in a challenging manner, so you want it to be as soft as you possibly can make it. However, the accuracy of the execution is of slightly greater significance. To reiterate, the point of a dink is to throw off your opponent and force them to make a mistake. Which of their two hands—their backhand or their forehand—do they use more effectively? You want to strike it on the side that has the lower defense. This requires a high level of accuracy.

You are free to execute a dinking stroke in any manner you see fit. Just keep in mind that you need to shoot with control, awareness, and concentration on the target. It calls for an extraordinarily high level of dexterity and accuracy. However, as is always the case, the more you use it, the better you will become at it.

7.2 The Fundamental Shots

Pickleball teaches a lot of different shots, but the fundamental ones are the ones you should focus on learning and perfecting first. Let's start with the fundamentals, shall we?

The serve

One of the most fundamental aspects of pickleball is the serve, which begins at each point. The shot is what kicks off the beginning of the point. It's not a volley and it's not a groundstroke either. It's only the serve at this point. There is a wide variety of ways in which one can be of service. It has a good degree of adaptability.

The Lob

The lob shot is among the most notorious shots in pickleball. In a lob shot, you send the ball into the air so that it flies over the heads of your competitors. Your competitors are compelled to turn around swiftly to chase the ball down in the backcourt. The abrupt change in tempo has the potential to make your opponent panic, which in turn increases their chances of making mistakes.

The lob shot is used nearly exclusively for one reason, and that is to aid in resetting the pace of a particular point. If the opposing team is hammering balls at you and you just can't reduce the pace of the game, you can use the lob shot to reset everything and get things back on track. If you hit the ball into the backcourt, your opponent will be forced to stay away from the net, giving you the chance to get to the net. However, you should not do this too often, because if you lob the ball too short, they might smash it back at you, and if you lob it too far, it might easily go out of the play area.

7.2.1 Cross-court Dink

A dink shot that goes from one corner of the pickleball court to the other corner of the opponent's court is referred to as a cross-court dink.

One of the pickleball shots with the most devastating impact is the dink that is played across the court. The fact that it is so difficult to master makes it one of the pickleball shots that can be the most frustrating to play. It is essential, however, to acquire the skills necessary to execute a cross-court dink and return the ball.

The most important thing is to have a good grasp of distance. A dink that is going in the direction that is directly in front of you will travel a shorter distance than one that is going in the direction that is going across the court. At the very least, it is twice as long. This indicates that you will need to apply a greater amount of force to move it. The cross-court dink can be executed in a variety of one-of-a-kind ways by different people. Nevertheless, how you go about taking this shot is entirely up to you. Always keep in mind that maintaining proper distance is the single most important factor.

7.2.2 The Drive

A volley or groundstroke that is hit at or close to the maximum amount of force possible is known as a drive. Drives are supposed to be difficult, fast, and impossible to halt. Drives are excellent for players with enough upper body strength, but they will be extremely hard for people who aren't strong. Drives are suitable for people with the upper body strength to do it. Drives should be viewed more as tools than as something to be used frequently as shots. Driving toward any of these positions will be effective if you notice an opening on the pickleball court or if the opposing team is running toward you.

But what are some ways to fight against a drive?

7.2.3 Put a dent in it

You can use the block shot in pickleball to prevent your opponent from gaining an advantage through drives, whether they are third-shot drives or regular drives. If the opposing team throws an aggressive shot at you, it's easy to make a mistake in your response. However, the block shot is available to assist.

The blocking shot is a very straightforward move to execute.

To execute a block shot, you need only bring your paddle around to your backhand side and hold it there. Nothing should be done besides watching the ball collide with the paddle. Do not attempt to hit it with your swing; this is the single most important point to keep in mind. Believe me when I say that the ball possesses a great deal of force and is aiming straight for you. You don't need to give it any more strength than it already has!

If you are successful in doing so, the ball will awkwardly enter the kitchen, making it hard for the opposing team to get it back. You can give your opponent less of an advantage in the game by blocking shots, which is also a good way to reduce the pace of the game.

7.2.4 Deep return serve

The deep return serve is an essential shot that needs to be mastered to be successful. It's not challenging, but it does take some time to master it efficiently.

When you hit the ball into the backcourt, it can be very difficult to gauge how far it travels. This is completely understandable. When we are attempting to judge great distances, our sense of depth becomes a little off-kilter. Finding a friend or pickleball partner and returning serves to them is the most effective way to train for this skill. They will then be able to tell you the length of your shot to assist you in figuring out how to win. Your brain will eventually form a pattern, and after some time you will become accustomed to it.

7.2.5 The Backhand Punch

The backhand punch is a nice shot that never fails to take the opponent by surprise. The backhand punch is a type of shot that is usually executed at the net and involves hitting the ball squarely. This shot is intended to convert a high dink made by the opposing team into a shot that goes directly at them.

It is not difficult to carry out. Simply place your paddle in the backhand position and make a fist as if you were going to punch something. Easy!

7.2.6 The Overhead Smash

This is without a doubt my favorite shot to play whenever I play pickleball. The overhead smash serves one purpose and one purpose only, and that is to annihilate the ball and make it unattainable for the opposing team to get it back. It's a good chance to take that shot.

If your rival pops up a shot that just barely sails over your head, this presents you with the perfect opportunity to seal the deal! Extend your hand and strike the ball in a downward direction. Accuracy is of the utmost importance here. Reduce the amount of wrist action you use if you're trying to hit the ball into the net. If, however, you are hitting the balls past the opponent's baseline, you should either increase the amount of wrist action you use or use a less heavier paddle

7.2.7 The Third Shot Drop

In pickleball, the most important shot to learn how to play is called the third shot drop. Learning how to execute this shot is necessary to play advanced pickleball. On the third shot, a significant number of points are dropped. The reason for this is that when players try to make this shot, they are under a great deal of pressure. Although you and your teammates are still at or near the baseline, the opposing team has already reached the non volley done and has a significant edge over you.

The third shot drops are gentle shots that travel upward before touching down gently in the kitchen. Your opponent will be forced to dink the ball rather than drive it as a result of the soft landing. Your opponent has the potential to smash or drive the ball if you hit your shot too high or too far, which increases the likelihood that you will lose the point.

Having someone positioned at the kitchen line is one of the most effective ways to hone your skills in the art of third-shot drops. Ask them to tell you where in the kitchen the ball landed each time you hit one so that you can get a sense of how far you are hitting it.

7.2.8 Centerline ace

Having a strong serve with topspin is typically required for this to be successful. If you don't, it's going to be very difficult to make it work. This particular serve is one of my favorites to play. It's a ton of fun, and I highly suggest practicing it in your free time.

The goal of this move is to hit the ball as aggressively as you can while applying as much topspin as you can while remaining precisely in the center of the court. If you are successful, your opponent might not even be able to move at all. It will race down the centerline at breakneck speed, leaving your opponent unable to respond.

7.2.9 The Dink Fake

This move is among the most cunning and underhanded shots you can make in pickleball. If executed properly, the dink fake is a particularly brutal move; however, it is not easy to pull off.

The dink fake occurs when you give the impression that you are going to dink a semi-high ball, and instead you drive the ball. It is unexpected, quick, and offers the possibility of a third shot drive if the return was inadequate.

Two things need to happen for the dink fake to work:

The height of the ball must be sufficient.

You need to have an adequate amount of topspin.

For this shot to be successful, the ball needs to be at a sufficient height; otherwise, it will go straight into the goal. On the other hand, you need to apply sufficient topspin to the ball so that it curves above the net and stays within the baseline.

This is the time where you muster up your acting skills and put them to use. You should first give the impression to the opposing team that you are going to dink the ball, and then all of a sudden drive it. The trick here is to make it look like it is materializing out of thin air. You want to take the opposing completely by surprise!

If you aim this shot directly at your opponent, it will be even more devastating to them.

7.2.10 Return of Serve With a Backspin

This shot is not only hilarious when performed perfectly, but it also has the potential to be very effective if it is used in the right way.

You must wait until a semi-high serve comes your way before you can perform this shot. When it seems to be pliable and straightforward, slice it straight downward using your paddle. The ball will rise into the air gently, but when it lands, it will have a significant amount of sidespin on it. It should be very difficult for the opposing team to return the ball if it bounces directly to the side. When executed flawlessly, the shot will hit either corner of the kitchen, then bounce off the ground and land on the side after traveling a distance of one foot.

It should come as no surprise that this attempt is fraught with peril. It can go out of bounds, enter the net, or become a regular return serve that doesn't do anything else other than to increase your chances of making a mistake. The spin will be even more extreme if you use a paddle that has a fiberglass face on it.

Shot taken around the goalposts

This is a one-in-a-million chance, but potentially lethal shot. When one considers the shot's scarcity and illustrious history, it is undeniably one of the most impressive. You will only have a chance to make this shot if the opposing team makes an aggressive shot across the court or a dink that bounces far away from your side of the court. The trick to succeeding in this endeavor is to run alongside the ball so that you can keep up with its speed. Since the ball has traveled a sufficient distance away from the sideline, you are allowed to touch it around the post lightly. After that, you will be able to bask in the waves of applause that will be washing over you from all directions.

It is crucial to keep in mind that even if the ball goes into the opposing team's half of the court after hitting the side post, you will still be penalized for the fault.

7.2.11Backhand spin dink

If you are fine with using a dinking stroke, you might want to consider changing it to a more sophisticated move once you've reached that level of comfort. This type of shot can only be successful if it is a backhand dink shot that is taken from the opposite side of the court. If your shot is right-handed, you'll be on the left corner of the pickleball court, and if you shoot left-handed, you'll be on the right.

If you feel comfortable enough to use it, this is a nice shot. The key is to move your body under the ball to generate a backspin. The opposing team will likely see your shot being taken and will be prepared for it; however, this does not mean that they will not make any errors.

This shot is tricky because the dink is typically easy to make, but the backspin makes everything a great deal more unpredictable. When attempting this shot, one of the most common errors is to hit it too high. You may stick with a standard cross-court dink if you are competing against tall players who have enormous wingspans.

8 LEARNING HOW TO PLAY PICKLEBALL

Learning pickleball takes a lot of dedication, patience, and commitment. Nowadays, there are various ways to learn pickleball. You can take lessons, attend clinics or get a personal coach.

While having lessons and attending clinics are great options, you have to ensure that you are learning from an excellent pickleball coach.

It can be challenging to locate qualified pickleball teachers and pickleball coaches. Most of them are formerly collegiate or high school players who appear capable of striking a ball. Still, they have little to no expertise in really instructing others.

They have rarely taken courses in the fundamentals of Pickleball, read books about correct moves, attended classes in the fundamentals of teaching techniques and pickleball coaching, or obtained certification from the Pro Pickleball Registry (PTR) or the United States Pickleball Teachers Association (USPTA) (US Pro pickleball Association).

Always ensure to ask potential pickleball coaches about their UTPR score, whether or not they have a national certification (and by what association and level: high, medium or low), if they have ever ranked high in the UTPR, how long they have been teaching professionally, the age limits and efficiency levels of their students, the kinds of places they have taught in (annual indoor centers or part-time summer camps), and the notable Pickleball authors they have been inspired by.

Also, try to get a sense of their professionalism, maturity level, dedication, personality type and their communication abilities (their ability to communicate effectively and clearly). All this should be done while talking to the potential pickleball coaches you'll be working with.

Since you are investing significant money in pickleball lessons, you have every right to anticipate positive progress very soon. Suppose you have trouble comprehending your pickleball instructors during your sessions and have made very little progress. In that case, you shouldn't cross your fingers, expecting that you will master all the skills one day and start making progress suddenly.

Expect to see results as you compete in the game. You should start seeing improvements after your first pickleball lesson and continue to see improvements after each subsequent pickleball class if your pickleball teachers are really as skilled as they profess to be.

The cost of hiring a qualified pickleball instructor is money well spent. A bad pickleball instructor is nothing more than a waste of your time and money.

8.1 Accreditation on a National Scale

Even though this accreditation does not ensure a GREAT pickleball coach, it does ensure a respectable baseline level of pickleball experience. Regrettably, the vast majority of pickleball coaches cannot fulfill this position's requirements.

Always make it a point to inquire about the possible pickleball instructors and coaches you're interested in hiring about their level of national certification.

The USPTA and the PTR are highly-respected certifying agencies in the United States that the USTA sanctions. Additionally, both organizations have certified pickleball coaches for nearly 35 years. Pickleball instructors can earn certifications in one of three generally escalating levels through the organization (low; medium; high).

Excellent pickleball play Coaches consistently put in a lot of work and research to ensure they can pass periodic reexaminations and maintain their certification at best possible level.

8.2 UTPR Score

Regardless of what a pickleball instructor might believe or claim, it is physically impossible for that individual to instruct you in a skill they do not already possess and so cannot teach.

If a pickleball instructor only has a UTPR rating of 4.0, then they are not qualified to teach you how to play at an NTRP rating of 4.5 or higher. It is entirely up to your abilities and not those of your pickleball teacher if you chance to progress to the point where you surpass your pickleball teacher's UTPR level.

Always inquire about the UTPR rating level of any possible pickleball teachers. It is poor judgment to accept a lower level of quality in exchange for a lower price. You won't gain much and you won't see significant results. It's better to set a high standard for yourself to ensure that you will make progress more quickly.

8.3 Certifications

Even though having a high USTA (United States pickleball Association) player rating is not a failsafe way to ensure receiving quality pickleball instruction, it is undeniably beneficial. It is best to steer clear of pickleball coaches who have never had a ranking or achieved a USTA rating in their careers.

Always inquire about the current and previous rankings held by any possible pickleball instructors—the greater the number, the better.

8.4 Years and Range of Experience

Experience can't be replicated by anything else. However, the experience of teaching pickleball can be achieved in several other contexts. These include indoor and outdoor facilities that are open throughout the year and outdoor institutions that are open only during the summer. Examples include children and adult camps, country clubs and recreation department programs. The experience of coaching pickleball that can be earned during a summer kids' camp is significantly less valuable than the experience gained at a club open all year. This will directly impact the effectiveness of your pickleball lessons.

Always ask potential pickleball instructors where they got their previous experience before hiring them.

8.4.1 Experience Working with Students of Varied Ages, Grades, and Group Sizes

Different ages and skill levels require various instructional tactics and strategies when teaching pickleball. Suppose the person you are considering hiring as your pickleball instructor has spent most of their time working with youngsters. In that case, it will be difficult for that person to give you the appropriate pickleball instruction you need as an adult. When compared to teaching in a group setting, instructing a single student one-on-one in a private setting calls for quite different and more challenging skills.

Always ask any possible pickleball instructors how much experience they have taught others of the same age and skill level as you, and if they have tutored groups or private sessions.

8.5 Expertise and Skill with the Correct Procedures

Knowledge is essential, and a fantastic pickleball instructor can only obtain it by devoting a significant amount of time and energy to furthering their education. They must have studied a large number and diversity of pickleball instruction books, watched an adequate number of instruction videos, and participated in several important pickleball instruction classes and workshops on the correct stroke technique. There is no easy way out of this situation.

Always inquire about the possible pickleball instructor's educational background before hiring them.

8.6 Communication Abilities

It doesn't matter how much your pickleball coach knows about the right way to play the game; if they can't explain it to you in a way that's easy to understand and doesn't waste your time, the information is pointless.

Always pay attention to how the potential pickleball instructor communicates with you while conversing with them. If you are unable to comprehend them at the initial phase of the discovery process, there is a good likelihood that you will be equally confused if the case is brought before a judge.

8.7 Personality

Even though personality comes up last in this list, its significance cannot be understated when compared to the other factors. A kind, outgoing, gregarious, timely, dependable, positive, encouraging, energetic and mature person, will give you a good time on the Pickleball court. Always keep in mind to look for these warm and welcoming qualities while you are having your initial conversation with someone about taking pickleball lessons.

CONCLUSION

Pickleball is a great sport. Though it's not as popular as tennis, it's gradually making its way into mainstream sports. Like all games, you need mental strategies and excellent techniques to win. If you want to learn pickleball or you want to get better at it, the strategies in this book will significantly help you achieve your goals.

Printed in Great Britain
by Amazon

17512749R00063